The Inheritance

KOOKOGEY™

NASHVILLE

Published by THE KOOKOGEY GROUP, 9050 Carothers Pkwy, Suite 104, #25, Franklin, TN 37067

www.kookogey.com

The KOOKOGEY name and logo are trademarks of THE KOOKOGEY GROUP, registration pending in the United States Patent & Trademark Office.

Kevin Kookogey is an entertainment lawyer who speaks and teaches on topics as diverse as music and entertainment, politics, western civilization and educa-tion. For more information or to book Mr. Kookogey for an event, please con-tact kevin@thekookogeygroup.com, or visit our website at www.kookogey.com

Cover Design by Kevin Kookogey and Marc Theodosiou

Illustrations by Chris Taylor

Art Direction by Kevin Kookogey
Special thanks to Jordan Mattison

9050 Carothers Pkwy, Suite 104 #25, Franklin, TN 37067

Manufactured in the United States of America

ISBN: 978-0-615-36603-6

Because every grand question has to be argued

afresh in every generation

$\mathbf{O}$nce upon a time...

In a distant
familiar
land

A child was born.

The circumstances
of
the child's birth
were
tumultuous.

After giving birth,
the mother died.

Fortunately for the child,
the mother left him
an abundant Inheritance.

Instructions
regarding the preservation
of the
Inheritance
were also left with the Son.

These instructions
had been given to the mother
by her parents,
who had received them
from their ancestors.

For generation
upon
generation,
these instructions
were effective
in
preserving
the
Inheritance.

17

Many family members
read the instructions.

Some
committed the instructions
to memory.

Others
preserved the instructions
by writing their thoughts about them
for future generations.

Still others
penned the instructions
into
poems and stories
about their Inheritance.

Yet in every generation,
some
ignored
the
instructions

Or tried to change them.

They
were smarter
than their relatives.

They spread their wisdom
to the entire family.

33

The results were not good.

Generations
were left
with
bad instructions
or
without any instructions at all.

The Inheritance was nearly lost.

But
this reinforced
the reliability of the instructions.

Like his ancestors,
the Son
initially embraced
his
Inheritance.

He understood
that his Inheritance
had to be cultivated to thrive.

It was hard work.

But the Son
took pride in his labor.

For
inspiration
and
guidance,
he referred to the instructions.

Consequently,
the Son grew strong
and
prosperous.

Out of his abundance,
the Son responded dutifully –
to God
and
to his neighbor.

He defeated tyranny
and
restored freedom
throughout
the
world.

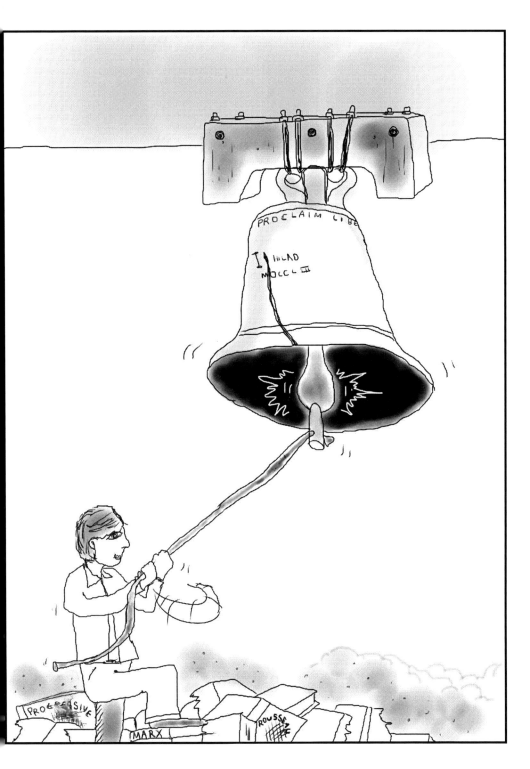

The Son believed
he had been given
a special destiny.

He was Exceptional.

He responded
when other families were in need.

He adopted children
from other families,
giving them
a share
in his
Inheritance,

And providing them
with the same instructions
his mother had given him.

The Son grew yet stronger
and more prosperous.

Rapidly.

Then the Son got married

To Success.

Success gave birth
to a Giant.

But Success
led to
unrealistic expectations

Of greater advances.

And perfection.

Now.

Success demanded
that the Son provide
for the Giant.

Impatient to appease Success,
the Son neglected the instructions

And lost his Inheritance.

Without an Inheritance,
the Son was unable
to provide for Success.

Or the Giant.

So he took from them

And
promised
to take care of them.

With bread

And circuses.

The Giant grew weak

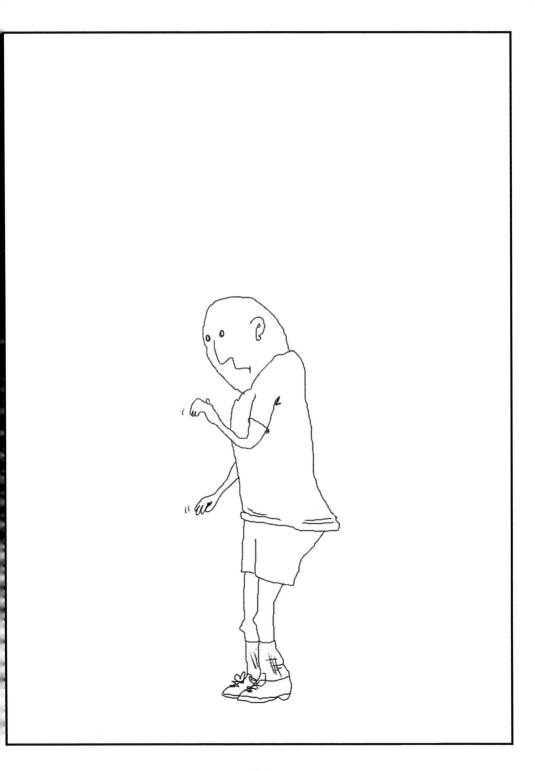

And dependent.

Success fell pregnant

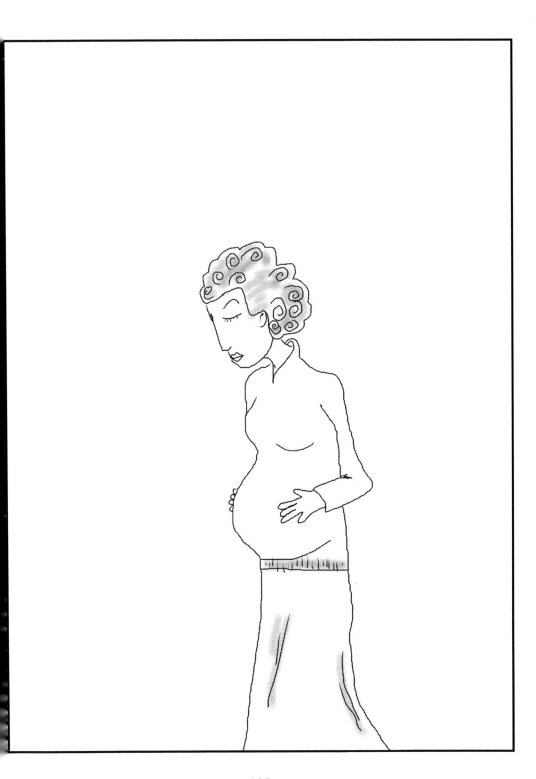

And died

While giving birth to Apathy.

Apathy corrupted
the vulnerable Giant.

In shame unaware,
the Giant fell asleep.

Apathy gave birth
to Dependency,
herself a wayward woman.

In time,
Dependency brought forth a son

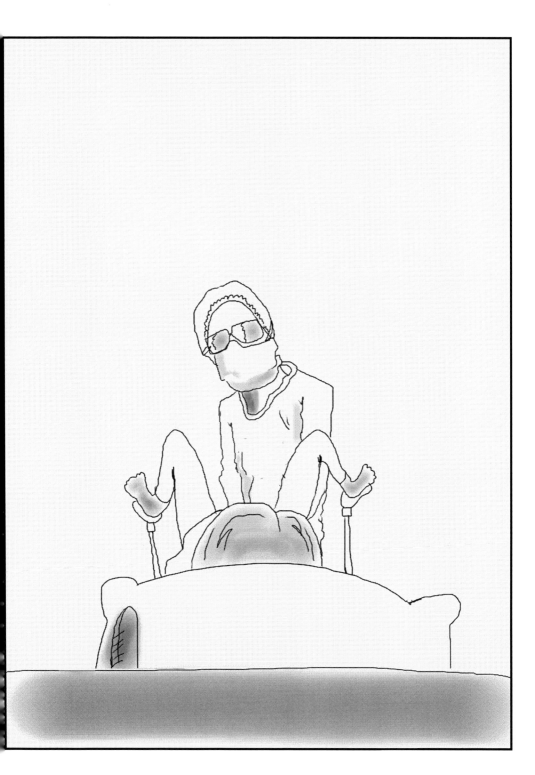

Whose name was Bondage.

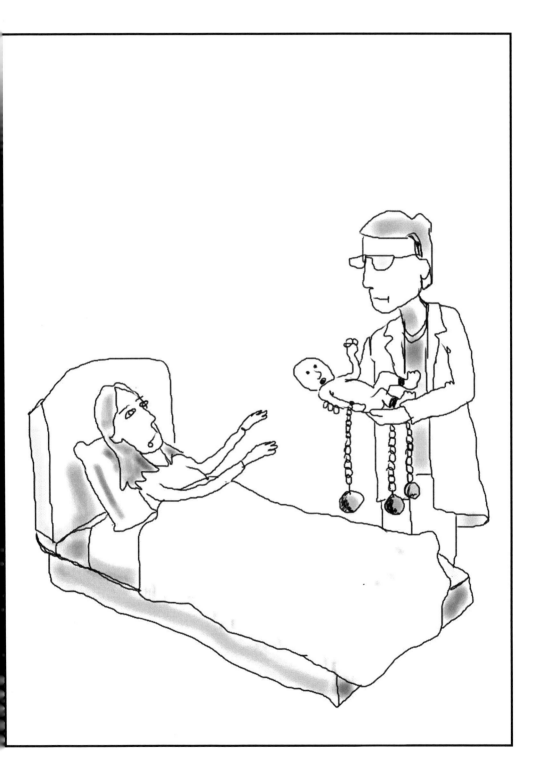

The sleeping Giant
was given over to Bondage.

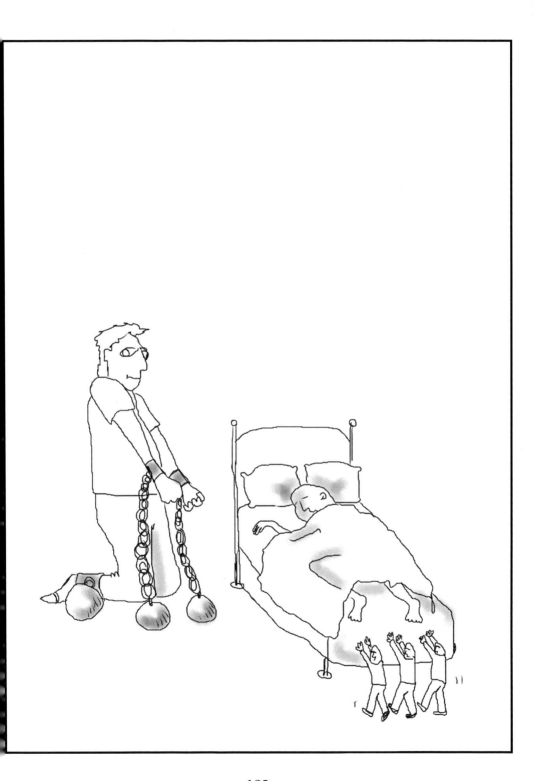

Then there arose
from a place unknown,
the
One
in whom much
hope
was
sown.

Bondage surrendered the Giant

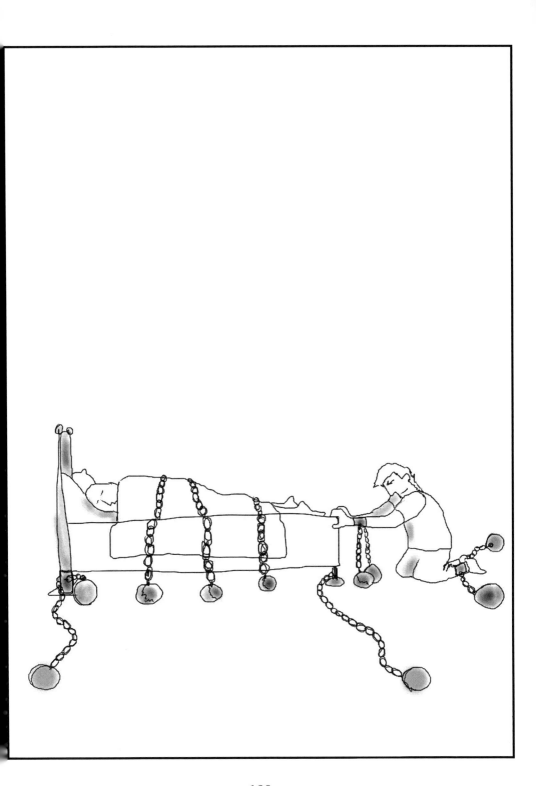

To the One.

Aroused by this,
the Giant reacted

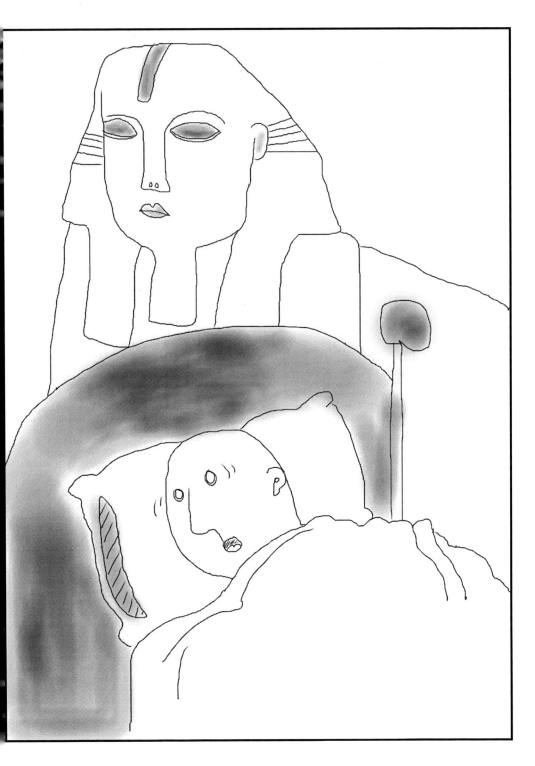

Impulsively.

Great was the battle.

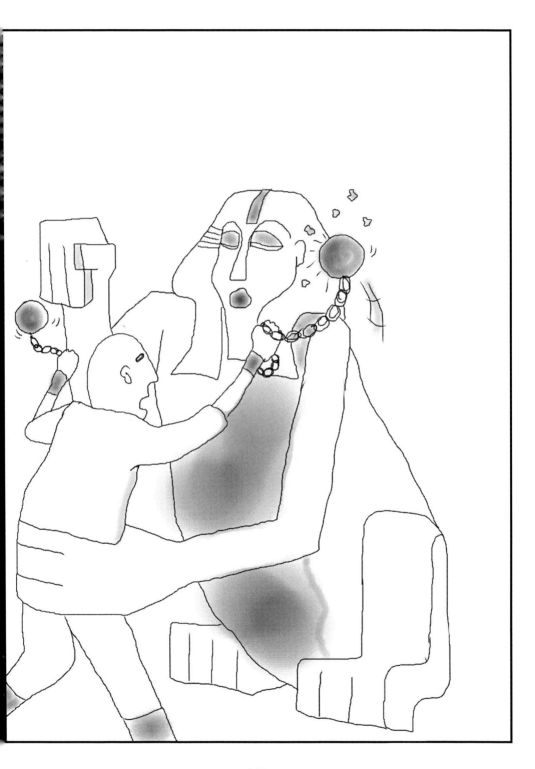

Brief were the gains.

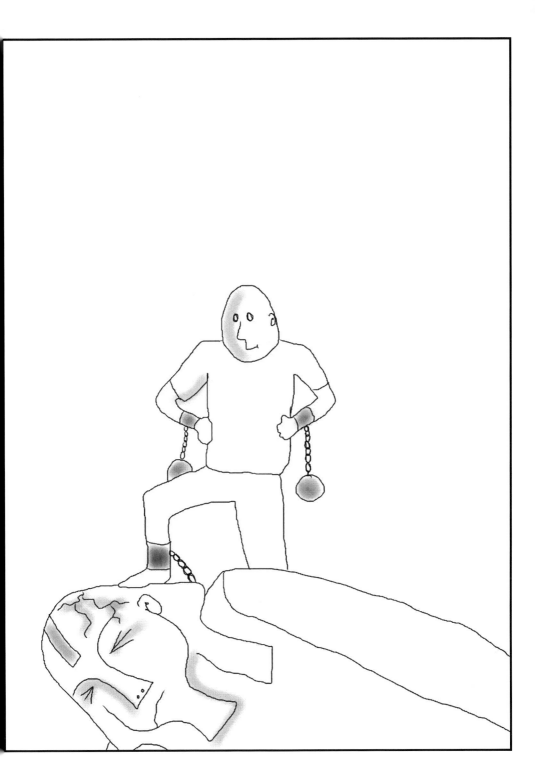

Without an Inheritance, the Giant was no match for the Change

Which took place
while the Giant slept.

Summoning up great courage,
the Giant determined to prepare

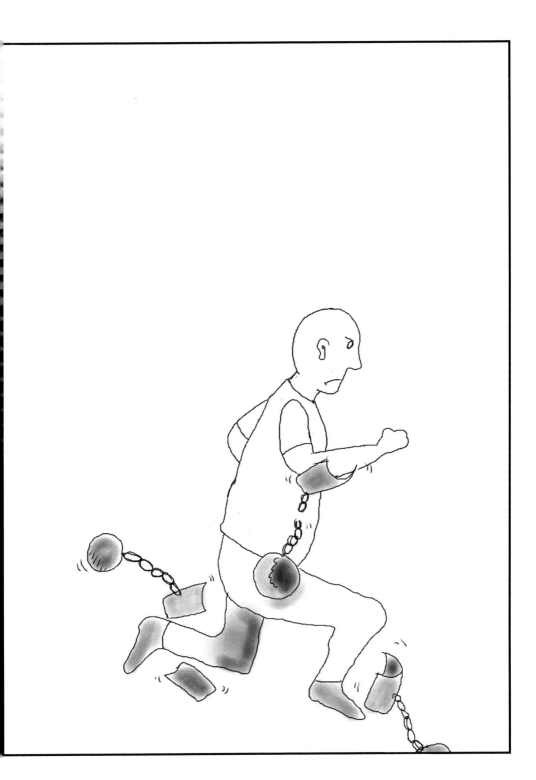

To restore his family tradition.

Dusting off
the ancient instructions,

The Giant learned
that his Inheritance was secure.

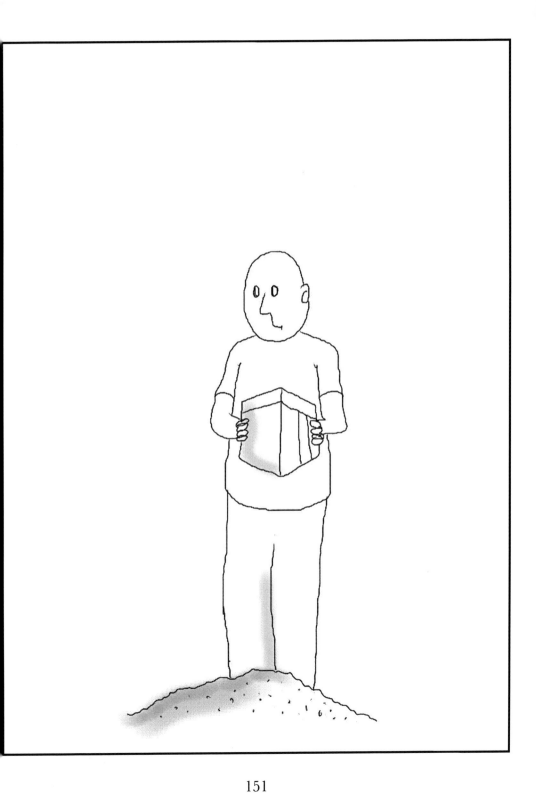

But it had to be cultivated to thrive.

It was hard work.

But the Giant
took pride in his labor.

For
inspiration
and
guidance,
the Giant referred
to
the
instructions.

The Inheritance
produced a great harvest,

Reviving the Giant

Who defeated the One,

Giving honor
Where honor was due.

The Giant
had
defeated tyranny
and
restored freedom to the Son.

The Son prospered once again.

The Giant knew
the Son had been given
a special destiny.

He was Exceptional.

Yet
dark clouds
billowed on the horizon.